扫描文章前的二维码
收听该故事的英文音频

"伟人的少年故事"丛书

科学的先驱

—— 推动科学方法诞生的奇才 ——

（斯里兰卡）努雷·维塔奇（Nury Vittachi） 著
斯泰帕·张（Step Cheung） 图
朱之翀 译　张 群 审校

上海科技教育出版社

图书在版编目(CIP)数据

科学的先驱：推动科学方法诞生的奇才/(斯里)努雷·维塔奇(Nury Vittachi)著；朱之翀译.—上海：上海科技教育出版社，2018.8

("伟人的少年故事"丛书)

书名原文：Scientific Pioneers

ISBN 978-7-5428-6713-1

I.①科… II.①努… ②朱… III.①科学家—生平事迹—世界—青少年读物 IV.①K816.1—49

中国版本图书馆CIP数据核字(2018)第069064号

Contents

Aglaonike The Woman Who Hid the Moon 3

Al-Haytham The Man Who Stayed in His House for Ten Years 10

Shen Kuo The Boy Who Was Curious All His Life 20

Hildegard of Bingen The Grumpy Nun Who Was Forbidden to Sing 27

Carl Linnaeus The Boy Who Sorted Out the Living World 35

Jean Piaget The Boy Who Found Different Ways of Thinking 42

Artemisia The Woman Who Taught Us Love and Remembrance 51

Lillian Gilbreth The Mother with Six Boys and Six Girls 59

Enheduanna The Girl Born in the Shadow of the Moon God 64

Alice Hamilton The Explorer Girl Who Travelled Far Without Leaving Home 71

目 录

阿格拉欧奈克　"藏起"月亮的女子　3

伊本·海赛姆　被禁锢了10年的男子　10

沈括　毕生追求知识的男孩　20

希尔德加德　被禁止唱圣歌的修女　27

卡尔·林奈　将生物分类的男孩　35

让·皮亚杰　发现了不同思维方式的男孩　42

阿尔特米西娅　教会我们爱和纪念的公主　51

莉莉安·吉尔布雷斯　六个男孩和六个女孩的母亲　59

思西壮安娜　出生于月神之影中的女孩　64

爱丽丝·汉密尔顿　在家远行的探险女孩　71

THE WOMAN WHO HiD THE MOON

阿格拉欧奈克
"藏起"月亮的女子

SOMETIMES YOU'D THINK IT would be **tough**① to be a girl in the old days. There was no such thing as "women's rights" and men were in charge of most things outside the home.

Yet we should not think that women were oppressed throughout history until modern times. Remember, human society itself **evolves**②, and in the long run we arrange things to the best advantage of all members of humanity, female and male.

If we study history, we notice that in every era, there were many women who did amazing things, and were often leaders, from Boudica (say "Bow-di-ka") in the UK to the Chinese Empress Xiaozhuangwen (say "She-ow, ju-ang, wen").

Here's a really interesting example. Some time in the second century BC, a woman named Hegetor had a daughter named Aglaonike (pronounced "Agla-o" and then "Ni-ke", like the sports shoe).

Aglaonike loved the sky and spent hours watching the movements of the stars. During the daylight hours, she would study the writings of the great thinkers of the times.

She lived in Greece. In those days, in the centuries before the birth of Christ, her homeland produced a huge number of the world's most important thinkers and greatest discoveries.

Aglaonike joined a group called The Witches of Thessaly, a group of clever women who were famous from the third century to the first century BC.

你可能会认为,古代女子的生活很艰难,那时没有"女权"之类的意识,男性掌控着家庭以外的大部分权力。

然而,我们不能就此认为,在现代社会之前的整个历史长河中,所有女性都一直处于备受压迫的地位。你要知道,人类社会本身是在进步的,从长远来看,一切事物的安排都是有利于所有人类成员的,无论男女。

如果我们研究历史,我们就能够注意到,无论什么时代,都有成就卓著的女性,她们通常还是领导者,比如英国的布狄卡(读作"Bow-di-ka")和中国的孝庄文皇后(读作"She-ow, ju-ang, wen")。

我们来看一个很有趣的例子。公元前2世纪的时候,有一位名叫荷格托的女子,她的女儿名叫阿格拉欧奈克(读作"Agla-o"和"Ni-ke",后一音节和运动鞋品牌同音)。

阿格拉欧奈克喜欢天空,她常常花好几个小时观察星星的运动。白天她就阅读当时伟大的思想家们的著作。

她生活在希腊。那时还是公元前,希腊已经涌现出了一大批世界上最伟大的思想家,作出了大量最重要的发现。

阿格拉欧奈克加入了一个叫作"赛萨利女巫"的组织,其成员均为公元前3世纪至公元前1世纪时才华横溢的女性。

---

① **tough** [tʌf] *adj.* 艰苦的、困难的、坚强的、不屈不挠的、坚韧的、牢固的、强壮的、结实的

② **evolve** [ɪ'vɒlv] *vt.* 发展、进化、使逐步形成、推断出;*vi.* 发展、进展、进化、逐步形成 [evolved, evolved, evolving]

Now it may seem odd to have someone whose title was "witch" in a science book. But remember, for most of history, people were very open-minded, and all sorts of different forms of knowledge were **blended**① together. And even today, open-mindedness is considered a key quality of a good scientist.

One day, Aglaonike realized something. From her sky charts, she knew that the moon would soon undergo an **eclipse**②.

The moon would begin its period in the sky looking like it was full, a bright disk.

But then the shadow of the earth would fall over it — and it would disappear as if someone was taking bites out of it.

She decided to make a big announcement, to **demonstrate**③ the power of knowledge. On a certain night soon **approaching**④, people could watch as a force would "take the moon down from the sky", she said.

Surely not!

How could such a thing happen?

Excitement spread and people gathered that night to watch. It was very dark: there were no lights of course, so they had candles and **torches**⑤, or just sat under the starlight (no light pollution or smog in those days, lucky them).

And just as Aglaonike had said, the moon began to disappear.

如今，如果一本科学著作中有人的头衔是"女巫"，你可能会觉得很奇怪。但你要记住，在大多数历史时期，人类是开明的，各种不同的知识形态混杂在一起。即使在现代社会，开放的思想也被认为是一位优秀科学家必备的重要品质。

※

一天，阿格拉欧奈克有了个新发现。她根据自己的星空图推断，月亮将发生一次月食。

月食开始前，月亮看起来像一个悬挂在空中的明亮的大圆盘。

但很快，地球的阴影将会遮住它——圆盘会消失，就像有人把其中的一部分拿走了似的。

阿格拉欧奈克决定隆重地宣布这一发现，向人们展示知识的力量。她说，就在即将到来的某个夜晚，人们将会看到有一股力量"把月亮从天空中摘下来"。

这当然是不可能的！

这种情况怎么可能发生呢？

消息很快传开。那个夜晚，人们兴奋地聚集在一起，抬头观望星空。天很黑——那时还没有电灯，人们举着蜡烛和火炬，有些人干脆在星光下席地而坐（他们很幸运，那个时代还没有光污染和烟雾）。

正如阿格拉欧奈克所言，月亮逐渐消失了。

① **blend** [blend] *vt.* 混合；*vi.* 混合、协调 [blended 或 blent, blended 或 blent, blending]
② **eclipse** [ɪ'klɪps] *n.* 日食、月食、黯然失色；*vt.* 使黯然失色、形成（日、月）食 [eclipsed, eclipsed, eclipsing]
③ **demonstrate** ['demənstreɪt] *vt.* 证明、展示、论证；*vi.* 示威 [demonstrated, demonstrated, demonstrating]
④ **approach** [ə'prəʊtʃ] *vt.* 接近、着手处理；*vi.* 靠近 [approached, approached, approaching]
⑤ **torch** [tɔːtʃ] *n.* 火把、火炬 [torches]

Her name became part of a popular **proverb**① in those days.

Say a person asked you to do something and you wanted to **emphasize**② your agreement. Instead of just nodding and saying "yes", you would say: "Yes, as the moon obeys Aglaonike."

在那个时代，她的名字成了一个流行语。

假如有人让你做一件事，而你想要强调自己同意，你不必只是点头，或对他说"好的"，你可以说："好的，就如同月亮服从阿格拉欧奈克那样。"

---

① **proverb** [ˈprɒvɜːb] n. 谚语、格言，众所周知的人或事
② **emphasize** [ˈemfəsaɪz] vt. 强调、着重 [emphasized, emphasized, emphasizing]

THE MAN WHO STAYED IN HIS HOUSE FOR TEN YEARS

伊本·淘赛姆
被禁锢了10年的男子

A LITTLE OVER ONE THOUSAND years ago, a **cross**[1], hard-hearted prince named Al-Hakim was born in Egypt. He became Caliph (which means "leader") at the age of 11, in the year 996 AD.

He was a tough person who had his critics put to death and churches destroyed.

People were **scared**[2] of him and worried about what he was doing to society.

The Caliph's wise man was so upset that he felt he was losing his mind and told his staff to lock him away.

For the next 10 years, the Caliph continued to rule the land in a **harsh**[3] way. When a barking dog kept him awake at night, he banished all dogs from the land. He did not like certain vegetables and shellfish, so he made them illegal.

Then one night, the Caliph went out on a **donkey**[4] by himself, as was his habit, and never returned. The donkey and a **blood-stained**[5] garment were found — so perhaps one of his citizens killed him.

The leaders of the community met to decide which of the princes should be the next leader.

But while this was taking place, something remarkable happened. Remember the Caliph's wise man, who had gone crazy?

一千多年前，埃及出生了一位性情乖戾而且铁石心肠的王子，他的名字叫哈基姆。哈基姆在公元 996 年，也就是 11 岁时成了哈里发（"统治者"的意思）。

　　他是一个冷酷的人，谁批评他，他就处死谁，教堂也被他毁掉了。

　　人们都很害怕他，担忧他会祸及全社会。

　　哈里发身边有一位智者，他终日惴惴不安，觉得自己的大脑出了问题，于是要求手下把他关了起来。

　　在接下来的 10 年里，哈里发继续用残酷的手段统治着这片土地。有条狗在夜里吠叫，把他吵醒了，他随即下令把所有的狗逐出埃及。他不喜欢某些蔬菜和贝类，于是就将它们列为违法食品。

　　一天晚上，哈里发独自一人骑驴出门——这是他的习惯，但再也没有回来。人们后来找到了那头驴和一件沾着鲜血的衣服——所以，很可能是某个平民杀了他。

　　埃及的统治者们聚集在一起，讨论决定由哪一位王子来担任下一任哈里发。

　　但就在他们讨论时，一件不寻常的事情发生了。你们还记得那位发疯的哈里发智者吗？

---

① **cross** [krɒs] *adj.* 交叉的、相反的、乖戾的、生气的
② **scare** [skeə] *vt.* 惊吓、把……吓跑；*vi.* 受惊；*n.* 恐慌、惊吓、惊恐 [scared, scared, scaring]
③ **harsh** [hɑːʃ] *adj.* 严厉的、严酷的，刺耳的、粗糙的、刺目的
④ **donkey** [ˈdɒŋkɪ] *n.* 驴子，傻瓜、顽固的人 [donkeys]
⑤ **blood-stained** 沾染着血的、血迹斑斑的

He asked to talk to the nobles and explained that he had not really gone crazy at all. His name was Ibn Al-Haytham, and he explained that the Caliph had given him an impossible assignment. He knew that he would fail and the punishment would be that he would be put to death.

So he had pretended to be mad, so that he would be locked up instead.

Al-Haytham turned out to be a very interesting person. He had been a Cairo-born youth of just 19 years old when the Caliph had been born.

Al-Haytham's interest had always been astronomy, and when he heard that the new young leader was also interested in science, he thought they would work together happily.

Al-Haytham had got a job as a wise man in the palace.

But the Caliph Al-Hakim had demanded that the young wise man oversee a project to turn the desert green.

Al-Haytham had studied the plans and realized that the project would fail — and failure always meant death.

So he had pretended to go mad.

What had Al-Haytham done for the 10 years he had spent in one house? "I did a lot of thinking, and experiments," he **revealed**. "And I wrote a book."

他要求与埃及的贵族们对话，告诉他们事实上自己根本没有发疯。他说自己的名字叫伊本·海赛姆（Ibn Al-Haytham），哈里发曾让他去完成一项不可能完成的任务。他知道自己注定失败，而等待自己的惩罚是被处死。

所以，他不得不假装发疯，把自己囚禁起来。

大家发现，海赛姆是一个非常有趣的人。他在开罗出生，当哈基姆出生时，他才19岁。

海赛姆对天文学很感兴趣，当他听说新的统治者也对科学感兴趣时，他认为他俩可以愉快地合作。

海赛姆得到了一份工作，在宫中担任智者。

但哈里发哈基姆要求这位年轻的智者监管一个把沙漠变为绿洲的项目。

海赛姆对这个项目进行了认真的研究，认为它必定以失败告终——而失败常常意味着死亡。

所以，他假装自己疯了。

在被监禁的10年中，海赛姆在屋子里做了些什么呢？"我进行了大量的思考与实验，"他透露道，"而且写了一本书。"

---

① reveal [rɪ'viːl] vt. 显示、透露、揭露、泄露

And what a book it was! Al-Haytham's work was called "The Book of **Optics**[1]" and it was a **masterpiece**[2], seven volumes long. It was all about light.

Al-Haytham had spent a lot of his time looking out of the window of the house in which he had been **imprisoned**[3]. He saw the bright noonday sun. He saw the interestingly hazy light of **twilight**[4]. He saw the colors of dawn and sunset. He saw rainbows after the rain. He saw the strange silvery-blue brightness of moonlight, which seemed to remove colours from the things on which it shone.

He made observations and then wrote about how light worked: how it travelled in straight lines but could be **distorted**[5] by glass and water; how colors worked; how things are **reflected**[6] in mirrors at certain angles; and how our eyes work.

Al-Haytham was very smart, and most of his findings were new, valuable pieces of information.

But this important **Islamic**[7] scientist did much more than just tell the world about light. He was so careful with his experiments and observations that he taught us about the importance of making **hypotheses**[8] and testing them before deciding they were facts which could be trusted. He was one of the **originators**[9] of what is now called the scientific method.

那是一本旷世奇书！书名叫《光学之书》，是一部长达七卷本的巨作，内容都是关于光的。

海赛姆花费大量的时间，透过禁闭室的窗户观察室外。他看到了正午时分明亮的太阳，黄昏时分有趣又朦胧的光线，日升日落时的不同颜色；他还看到了雨后的彩虹，奇怪的银蓝色月光——仿佛把它所照耀的物体的颜色都抹去了。

他作了大量的观察，然后写下了关于光线的一些原理：光线如何沿直线传播，遇到玻璃和水如何产生折射；颜色如何形成；物体如何以特定的角度在镜中成像；我们的眼睛如何工作……

海赛姆非常睿智，他的大多数发现都蕴含着新颖而又极具价值的信息。

但是，这位重要的穆斯林科学家所作的贡献，远不止向世界传播关于光的知识。他对实验和观察的严谨态度告诉我们：作出假设，检验假设，然后确定其真实性，这是极其重要的。他是科学方法的创始人之一。

① **optics** [ˈɒptɪks] *n.* 光学
② **masterpiece** [ˈmɑːstəpiːs] *n.* 杰作、绝无仅有的人
③ **imprison** [ɪmˈprɪz(ə)n] *vt.* 监禁、关押、使……下狱
④ **twilight** [ˈtwaɪlaɪt] *n.* 黎明、黄昏、薄暮、衰退期、朦胧状态
⑤ **distort** [dɪˈstɔːt] *vt.* 扭曲、使失真、曲解；*vi.* 扭曲、变形
⑥ **reflect** [rɪˈflekt] *vt.* 反映、反射、照出、表达、显示、反省；*vi.* 反射、映现、深思
⑦ **Islamic** [ɪzˈlæmɪk] *adj.* 伊斯兰教的、穆斯林的
⑧ **hypothesis** [haɪˈpɒθɪsɪs] *n.* 假设 [hypotheses]
⑨ **originator** [əˈrɪdʒɪneɪtə(r)] *n.* 发起人, 起源、起因

The history of science includes **contributions**[1] from all the main cultures of the world, and **Muslim**[2] scientist Al-Haytham is one who will always be remembered — even if he spent a big portion of his life as a crazy locked-up **lunatic**[3].

科学史见证了全世界所有重要文化作出的贡献，穆斯林科学家海赛姆将会永远被世人所铭记——即使他一生中有很长一段时间被当作疯子囚禁着。

① **contribution** [kɒntrɪˈbjuːʃ(ə)n] *n.* 贡献、捐献，投稿
② **Muslim** [ˈmʊzlɪm] *n.* 穆斯林、穆罕默德信徒；*adj.* 伊斯兰教的
③ **lunatic** [ˈluːnətɪk] *adj.* 疯狂的、精神错乱的，愚蠢的

THE BOY WHO WAS CURIOUS ALL HIS LIFE

沈括
毕生追求知识的男孩

OH BOTHER! SHEN KUO was sick again. The little boy was always getting some illness or another. He was stuck at home, day after day, feeling bad.

His parents, minor government workers, were not rich, but could afford to hire doctors to give him health potions, and fengshui experts to make sure he was sleeping in the right place.

But despite not having riches or health, little Shen Kuo had something else that would change the world: he had an **enormous**[1] sense of curiosity.

Why this? Why that? Why the other?

When doctors fed him foul medicines, he wanted to know what was in them and what they did. And when the fengshui master knew which way was south, the boy asked: "But how do you know?"

Curiosity can be a good thing for a student to have, and when Shen Kuo recovered, he did very well in his exams. His community, in the seaside town of Xiamen on the coast of China in the 1040s, congratulated him.

When Shen Kuo reached his 20s, he no longer became ill regularly, but still had his sense of curiosity. When faced with a problem of dealing with **swampland**[2] on assignment for the local government, he studied the problem and made a **drainage**[3] system which turned it into the finest farmland.

He zoomed up the ladder and became famous as a **polymath**[4], which is a person who is brilliant at a wide range of things, from poetry to science.

哦，真讨厌！沈括又生病了。这个小男孩身体很弱，经常生病，只好天天待在家里。

他的父辈都是朝廷官员，但级别不高，因此家境并不富裕，所幸还请得起医生为他开方治病，也能够请来风水师，确保沈括的居住环境有益于健康。

尽管富有和健康不属于他，但小沈括拥有一种可以改变世界的能力：强烈的求知欲。

为什么是这个？为什么是那个？为什么是其他？

当医生让他服用一些味道难闻的药物时，他就会问这些药物的成分是什么，又是如何发挥作用的。当风水师指出哪个方位是南方时，沈括便会问他："你是怎么知道的？"

对于学生来说，拥有求知欲是一件好事。身体好转后，沈括在每一次考试中都取得了优异的成绩。当时是 11 世纪 40 年代，他生活在中国浙江省的一座沿海小县城里。邻居们都恭喜他。

---

20 多岁后，沈括身体有所好转，但求知欲依然不减当年。当地官府委派他一项工作，解决沼泽地问题。他经过仔细研究，设计出一种排水系统，将沼泽地变成了一片优质农田。

他的名气越来越大，成了一位著名的博学家，从诗歌到科学……他在各个不同领域都有杰出表现。

---

① **enormous** [ɪˈnɔːməs] *adj.* 庞大的、巨大的
② **swampland** [ˈswɒmplænd] *n.* 沼泽地
③ **drainage** [ˈdreɪnɪdʒ] *n.* 排水、排水系统，污水
④ **polymath** [ˈpɒlɪmæθ] *n.* 博学的人；*adj.* 博学的

One day, as an adult, he sat in his garden at his home and wrote a book called "Dream Pool Essays", about all the things he was curious about. It featured discoveries ranging from "How the Sun Makes Rainbows" to "How to Use a Mineral Called Orpiment to Rub Out Mistakes on Paper." He said there was such a thing called "Dragon Fire", a type of **blaze**[1] which burned more brightly when you poured water on it. It sounds strange, but he was right — think of **petrol**[2] fires, or **chip-pan**[3] fires.

But he never forgot the things that made him curious when he was a child. So he wrote about how medicines worked.

And he also wrote the first known scientific description of how to make a compass, a secret that fengshui masters had known for centuries. **Geomancers**[4] would rub the tip of a needle with a rock called a **lodestone**[5] and dangle it from a single thread of silk tied halfway along it. Like magic, the needle would always find south. (Traditionally, Western compasses are made to point north, while Chinese ones are made to point south.)

By the year 1111, Chinese sailors were using compasses to find their way around the world, and they spread around the world to become one of the most important tools ever.

Shen Kuo's book taught us a lot of things. But it was his life that taught us the biggest lesson: Never lose the curiosity that you had as a child.

沈括成年后，有一天他坐在自家花园里，开始撰写《梦溪笔谈》，记录下所有令他深感好奇的事物，从"太阳下彩虹如何形成"到"如何用雌黄这种矿物擦去纸上的错字"……凡此种种，应有尽有。沈括在书中说，有一种火焰叫"龙火"，如果向它泼水，它反而会烧得更旺。这听起来很奇怪，但他说的没错——汽油或平底锅起火就是如此。

沈括从未忘记小时候就倍感好奇的两个问题（前文已有提及），所以他写下了药物的作用原理。

他还记录了指南针的制作方法，这是迄今历史上最早的科学文献。风水师们数百年前就知道了这个秘密。他们用天然磁石摩擦针尖，并把一根丝线系在针的正中间，然后把针悬挂起来。就好像变魔术一般，这根针将始终指向南方。（西方的指南针习惯上设计成指向北方，而中国的则指向南方。）

1111年，中国水手开始使用指南针确定环球航行的路线，指南针由此传到了世界各地，成为有史以来最重要的工具之一。

沈括的著作教给了我们很多知识，但他的人生经历教给了我们更重要的知识：永远不要失去你在孩提时代所拥有的那份求知欲。

① **blaze** [bleɪz] *vt.* 在树皮上刻路标、公开宣布；*vi.* 燃烧、照耀、发光、激发 [blazed, blazed, blazing]
② **petrol** ['petr(ə)l] *n.*（英）汽油
③ **chip pan** 深平底锅
④ **geomancer** ['dʒiːəʊmænsə] *n.* 风水师
⑤ **lodestone** ['ləʊdstəʊn] *n.* 天然磁石、吸引人的东西（等于 loadstone）

THE GRUMPY NUN WHO WAS FORBIDDEN TO SING

希尔德加德
被禁止唱圣歌的修女

CHRISTIANS TRADITIONALLY GIVE 10 per cent of everything they get to the local church.

So when a Christian family had their 10th child, they decided to give the entire girl as a gift to the local **monastery**① !

That might sound like an odd thing to do, but the girl herself was delighted. Her name was Hildegard of Bingen, and she was very spiritual.

Despite being only seven years old, she was keen to devote her life to the big questions of life.

In the year 1106 she arrived at an ancient monastery in Germany and started training to be a nun (think of Julie Andrews in the movie "The Sound of Music").

It **suited**② her perfectly, and by the time Hildegard was an adult, she was the head of the women's section, with the title of **Abbess**③ .

But all her life, Hildegard had an independent **streak**④ .

One day, she decided that women should have a separate monastery, because men were so bossy.

So she announced that she was "very firm" about her decision to move to her own building, and pretended to have turned to stone. She just sat there. She refused to move a muscle until the head abbot said yes.

按照传统，基督徒会将自己财物的十分之一赠予当地的教堂。

所以，一个信奉基督教的家庭生下第十个孩子后，他们决定把这个女孩作为礼物，送给当地的修道院！

这种行为听起来匪夷所思，但这个女孩自己却很高兴。她名叫希尔德加德（Hildegard），住在德国的宾根，精神很高尚。

尽管只有七岁，希尔德加德渴望把自己的一生投入到解决人生的重大问题中。

※ ❦ ※

1106年，她来到德国的一所古老的修道院，开始接受培训，准备当一名修女（想想电影《音乐之声》里的朱莉·安德鲁斯）。

希尔德加德非常适合做修女。成年后，她成为一名女修道院院长，管理女性部门。

终其一生，希尔德加德始终坚守独立自主的精神。

她认为男性太专横，有一天，她作了个决定：女性应该拥有一所自己的修道院。

于是，她宣布要搬到属于自己的修道院去，为了表明"坚定的"决心，她假装自己变成了石头，静静地坐着，一动不动，一直坐到男修道院院长同意她的要求为止。

---

① **monastery**［ˈmɒnəst(ə)rɪ］n. 修道院、僧侣［monasteries］
② **suit**［sjuːt; suːt］n. 套装、西装、一套外衣；vi. 合适、相称；vt. 适合、使适应
③ **abbess**［ˈæbes］n. 女修道院院长、女庵主持
④ **streak**［striːk］n. 条纹、线条、倾向、(性格上的)特色、性情、气质

So she became chief of her own all-girl monastery, and there she wrote many books about science and music and religion and nature — all of which were a single subject in those days. This was in the 1100s, when few people were recording knowledge in books.

Even when Hildegard was an old woman in her 80s, she still had a **naughty**[1] streak.

A man who had **misbehaved**[2] died and she showed him forgiveness, agreeing to give him a burial space.

But this was against the rules. Local church bosses said they would dig him up again. But they couldn't because she refused to tell them where he was buried.

"I've hidden him," she laughed.

Furious, they **excommunicated**[3] her whole monastery and made a rule forbidding her and the other women to ever sing again.

Now that was a sad, silent time for the women's monastery.

But Hildegard wrote to the church's top bosses, who thought she was a smart, good person, and forgiving the **evildoer**[4] was the Christian thing to do. They overturned the **verdict**[5] of the local chiefs.

Now she and "her girls" could sing once more.

最后，她成为一所其成员全部为女性的修道院院长，并在那里写下了许多关于科学、音乐、宗教和自然的著作——那时这四个领域同属一个学科。在 12 世纪，几乎还没有人把知识记录成书。

✦✦✦

即使到了 80 多岁，希尔德加德仍然很顽皮。

有一个品行不端的男子去世了，作为修女希尔德加德宽恕了他，同意为他提供安葬之处。

但这是违反规定的。当地教堂的主教们表示，他们要把这个男子的尸体挖出来。但他们没有成功，因为希尔德加德拒绝告诉他们尸体的埋葬地。

她笑道："我把他的尸体藏起来了。"

气急败坏的主教们把希尔德加德修道院中的所有修女都逐出了教会，并且下令，从此禁止她和修女们唱圣歌。

对于这所女性修道院来说，这是一段悲伤、寂静的日子。

希尔德加德给教会的最高领袖写了一封信。教会的最高领袖认为希尔德加德是一位既聪颖又善良的人，而原谅作恶者又正是基督徒所应该做的，于是推翻了当地主教们的判决。

从此，她和修道院里"她的女孩们"又能够唱圣歌了。

---

① **naughty** ['nɔːtɪ] *adj.* 顽皮的、淘气的、不听话的、下流的 [naughtier, naughtiest]
② **misbehave** [ˌmɪsbɪ'heɪv] *vi.* 作弊、行为不礼貌；*vt.* 使举止失礼、使行为不端 [misbehaved, misbehaved, misbehaving]
③ **excommunicate** [ˌekskə'mjuːnɪkeɪt] *vt.* 逐出教会、把……逐出教会；[excommunicated, excommunicated, excommunicating]
④ **evildoer** ['iːv(ə)ldʊə] *n.* 为恶者、做坏事的人
⑤ **verdict** ['vɜːdɪkt] *n.* 结论、裁定

After Hildegard died, people discovered that as well as the expected **hymns**[1] and plays, she had written many books of knowledge — and she went down in history as an important early scientist. She wrote a lot about herbs and medicinal plants, and her work influenced the way that people think about natural elements as the best sort of medicine there is.

Today, there are more women than men in spiritual groups, and many people like to remember Hildegard, the tough, cheeky visionary who started life as a gift to the church, and ended it as a gift to humanity.

在希尔德加德去世以后，人们发现，除了已知的赞美诗和剧本以外，她还撰写了大量其他方面的著作。她作为早期历史上一位重要的科学家而被载入史册。她的著作中含有大量关于草药和药用植物的内容，从中人们发现，自然界中的天然成分才是最好的药物。

　　如今，在各种宗教团体中，女性的人数超过了男性，很多人都乐于纪念希尔德加德——一位坚强而大胆的梦想家。她的一生，从作为礼物赠予教会开始，最终又以作为礼物赠予全人类而结束。

① **hymn** [hɪm] *n.* 赞美诗、圣歌、欢乐的歌

THE BOY WHO SORTED OUT THE LIVING WORLD

卡尔·林奈
将生物分类的男孩

THREE HUNDRED YEARS AGO, there lived a poor church **pastor**① called Linnaeus who had a little boy called Carl. The garden outside their house **sloped**② down to a lake.

The churchman often combined his main sources of pleasure, by sitting with his son in the garden, teaching him about the different parts of a flower.

Little Carl was **inspired**③, and by the age of eight, he could describe all 400 plants in his father's collection.

At first, the pastor was very proud of his son. But then the boy's enthusiasm for nature became a problem.

Carl had no interest in his school lessons — he just wanted to spend his time exploring the forests.

When the boy was 10, the pastor saved up enough money to send him to a school far away from the local **woodlands**④ of the place where they lived in Sweden.

But the boy soon found an interesting piece of woodland near the school, and preferred to spend his time there, instead of studying his books.

His parents were worried. They hoped that Carl would become a pastor and take over his father's job — but how could a man earn a living if he knew nothing but varieties of flowers?

三百年前，有一位贫穷的牧师叫林奈，他有一个儿子叫卡尔。他们家的房子外面有一个花园，沿着花园往下走是一条湖泊。

　　牧师经常和儿子一起，坐在花园里，教儿子认识不同的花卉……这成了他快乐的主要来源。

　　这些活动激发了小卡尔的兴趣，8 岁时，他就能够识别所有父亲收集的 400 种植物了。

　　最初，林奈为儿子的行为感到很骄傲。但很快，卡尔对大自然的这种热情变成了一个问题。

　　卡尔对学校课程毫无兴趣——他只想把时间花在探索森林上。

❦❦❦

　　卡尔一家住在瑞典，在卡尔 10 岁时，林奈攒够了钱，把儿子送进了一所学校，远离了他们家附近的森林。

　　但卡尔很快就在学校旁边找到了一片有趣的林地。相比于读书，他更喜欢待在那片树林中。

　　他的父母对此忧心忡忡。他们希望卡尔长大后能够成为牧师，接替父亲的工作——一个除了各种植物以外一无所知的人以后如何生存呢？

---

① **pastor** ['pɑːstə] *n.* 牧师；*vt.* 作……的牧师
② **slope** [sləʊp] *vi.* 倾斜；*vt.* 倾斜、使倾斜 [sloped, sloped, sloping]
③ **inspire** [ɪn'spaɪə] *vt.* 激发、鼓舞、启示、产生、使产生灵感 [inspired, inspired, inspiring]
④ **woodland** ['wʊdlənd] *n.* 林地、森林

Then a teacher at school realized that the fact that Carl preferred the forest to books might not be a bad thing. Perhaps he could become a **botanist**[①], which is an expert on plants.

By the time the boy was 17, Carl was reading strange, ancient "books of **herbs**[②]" day and night.

And when he went to university, he **devised**[③] a system of **classification**[④]: a way of listing living things according to the shapes and functions of their parts.

Using his system, you could pick up any plant in the world and work out which family it belonged to, how it would reproduce itself and so on.

By the time he was an adult, he became interested in animals too, and worked out a way to classify them as well.

He did the job so well that the Linnaeus system came to be used by scientists all over the world to preserve their knowledge of the living world.

One of the things scientists do, following Carl Linnaeus' system, is to declare one example of each plant or animal as the **Type Specimen**[⑤] and describe it in an official record.

后来学校里的一位老师意识到,卡尔对于森林的热爱并不一定是件坏事。他可能会成为一位植物学家。

17岁时,卡尔夜以继日地阅读奇怪的关于草药的古籍。

进入大学后,卡尔设计出了一种分类系统:根据植物各部位的形状和功效,将它们编列成表。

利用这一系统,无论我们采摘到世界上什么植物,都可以搞清楚它所属的科类、繁殖方式,等等。

成年后,卡尔开始对动物产生兴趣,并设计出同样一种列表,对动物进行分类。

卡尔的分类方式取得了巨大成功,全世界的科学家都开始使用林奈系统来保存他们所掌握的关于生物世界的知识。

根据卡尔·林奈(Carl Linnaeus)的分类系统,科学家们要做的一件事是,从每种动植物中找出一个样本作为模式标本,进行详细描述并作为官方文献标准。

---

① **botanist** [ˈbɒtənɪst] *n.* 植物学家
② **herb** [hɜːb] *n.* 香草、药草
③ **devise** [dɪˈvaɪz] *vt.* 设计、想出、发明 [devised, devised, devising]
④ **classification** [ˌklæsɪfɪˈkeɪʃ(ə)n] *n.* 分类、类别、等级
⑤ **type specimen** (生物学)模式标本、典型标本、原始标本

If you look up the official science records for the Type Specimen for a species known as **Homo sapiens**[1] (yes, that's you and me), you'll find a description of a certain Swedish man with fair hair and brown eyes.

Yes, the first scientifically classified human being was Carl Linnaeus himself!

如果你查找官方文献中智人种（没错，就是我们人类）的模式标本，你看到的是一位金发棕瞳的瑞典男子。

是的，第一个被科学分类的人就是卡尔·林奈本人！

---

① ***Homo sapiens*** 智人（现代人的学名）、人类

THE BOY WHO FOUND DIFFERENT WAYS OF THINKING

让·皮亚杰
发现了不同思维方式的男孩

ABOUT 100 YEARS AGO, a boy called Jean Piaget sat and watched his mother. She was very clever, but he thought she often worried too much about unimportant things.

He never worried at all, and he was happiest when he was doing his **hobby**①, which was collecting shells.

He loved his hobby so much that he contacted the local museum in his hometown of Neuchâtel in Switzerland for permission to visit after hours and look at the **mollusks**② (that's the scientific name for creatures like **clams**③, and **squid**④ and **snails**⑤).

But when he was about 10 or 11, he started thinking in a different way. He still didn't worry like his mother did, but he began to think in an **analytical**⑥ way, like an adult.

By the time Jean Piaget was 13, he was writing lots of scientific papers about mollusks and sending them to science **journals**⑦. They printed them, not realizing that he was a child. They probably thought he was Professor of Snails at some university!

As you can imagine, this bright young man did well at school and university, and when he was in his 20s, he ended up helping a friend mark a large group of test papers.

大约100年前，一个名叫让·皮亚杰（Jean Piaget）的男孩静静地坐在那里，一直观察着他的母亲。母亲非常聪明，但皮亚杰认为她总是为琐事操太多的心。

而他自己什么事都不操心。捡贝壳时他最开心，因为那是他的爱好。

他非常热爱捡贝壳，因此他联系了自己家乡——瑞士的纳沙泰尔市——一家博物馆，希望能够得到准许，在业余时间去参观那里的贝壳类软体动物（那是蛤蚌、乌贼和蜗牛等生物的学名）。

大约十一二岁时，皮亚杰开始用一种不同的方式进行思考。他仍然不会像母亲那样忧心忡忡，但他开始运用分析思维方式，就像成人一样。

13岁时，他写了很多关于贝壳类软体动物的科学论文，并把它们寄给了科学杂志。他们发表了他的论文，并没有意识到作者让·皮亚杰是个小孩。他们很可能认为他是某个大学研究软体动物的教授！

正如你所猜想到的，这位聪明的年轻人在中小学和大学期间非常优秀。20多岁时，有一次他帮助朋友批阅大量的试卷。

---

① **hobby** ['hɒbɪ] *n.* 嗜好、业余爱好 [hobbies]
② **mollusk** ['mɒləsk] *n.* [无脊椎] 软体动物
③ **clam** [klæm] *n.* 蛤、沉默寡言的人、钳子
④ **squid** [skwɪd] *n.* 鱿鱼、乌贼、枪乌贼 [squids 或 squid]
⑤ **snail** [sneɪl] *n.* 蜗牛、迟钝的人
⑥ **analytical** [ænə'lɪtɪk(ə)l] *adj.* 分析的、解析的，善于分析的
⑦ **journal** ['dʒɜːn(ə)l] *n.* 日报、杂志、日记、分类账

While Jean was **grading**[①] the answers, he noticed something. Children always made the same mistakes, and they were consistently different from the mistakes that teenagers and adults made.

And that was when he had the idea that would make him famous.

The mistakes that children made were not really wrong. They were right for the type of "**logic circuits**[②]" in their brains. Their minds worked differently.

But at a certain age, their brains would start working like those of adults, and they would switch to giving the answers that adults gave.

Jean Piaget also thought about his mother. He realized that clever adults often worried too much, and he discovered the **psychological**[③] term for it: she was **neurotic**[④].

These thoughts inspired him to become a **psychologist**[⑤].

He became a world expert on something called developmental psychology, specializing in the difference between children's brains and adults' brains.

He taught teachers that it was wrong to educate children as if they were little adults, making them sit in rows and take notes for hours.

Children learned through playing and having fun and using their imaginations.

皮亚杰在打分时注意到了一个现象：孩子们经常犯同样的错误，而那些错误总是和青少年、成年人犯的错误不同。

就在这时，他产生了一个想法，正是这个想法使他在后来的日子里名闻天下。

孩子们犯的错误不是真正的错误。对于他们大脑中的"逻辑回路"来说，它们是正确的。孩子们的思维方式与成人是不同的。

但到了一定的年龄后，他们的大脑开始像成年人一样思考，思维方式发生转变，从而给出成人式的答案。

让·皮亚杰想到了他的母亲。他意识到聪明的成年人经常忧心忡忡，他发明了一个心理学术语来描述这种现象：神经质。

这些想法激励他成为一名心理学家。

他成了一名发展心理学方面的世界级专家，专攻孩子和成人的大脑差异。

他告诉老师们，把孩子当作年幼的成年人来教育，让他们排排坐、连续记几个小时的笔记，这种做法是错误的。

孩子们是通过玩耍、享受乐趣和运用想象力来学习的。

---

① **grade** ［greɪd］ *n.* 年级、等级、阶段；*vt.* 评分、把……分等级；*vi.* 分等级［graded, graded, grading］
② **logic circuit** 逻辑回路
③ **psychological** ［ˌsaɪkəˈlɒdʒɪk(ə)l］ *adj.* 心理的、心理学的、精神上的
④ **neurotic** ［njʊəˈrɒtɪk］ *adj.* 神经过敏的、神经质的；*n.* 神经病患者、神经过敏者
⑤ **psychologist** ［saɪˈkɒlədʒɪst］ *n.* 心理学家、心理学者

One of the reasons why classrooms around the world today include toys and games and storybooks and paintings and colorful **posters**[1] is because of the findings of Jean Piaget.

Does your teacher sometimes tell you stories, or encourage you to draw pictures or do craft activities or play games? She may not know it, but she's putting into practice what Jean Piaget discovered.

如今，全世界的教室里都有玩具、游戏产品、故事书、绘画以及多彩的海报，而布置成这样的原因之一，就是让·皮亚杰作出的上述发现。

有时候，你的老师是不是会给你讲故事、鼓励你画画、做手工或者玩游戏？她可能自己都没有意识到，她这样做，正是在把让·皮亚杰的发现付诸实践。

① **poster** [ˈpəʊstə] *n.* 海报、广告、招贴

THE WOMAN WHO TAUGHT US LOVE AND REMEMBRANCE

阿尔特米西娅
教会我们爱和纪念的公主

ARTEMISIA WAS A PRINCESS. Cool job? Maybe not.

In the old days, princesses had few choices in their lives — and could not even choose who to marry. Love was not considered something to take seriously.

Princesses were given in marriage by their families to other rich families, to **seal deals**[1]. Romance was never part of the deal.

✧✧✧

But Artemisia the Second of Caria, a place which is now in a country called **Turkey**[2], was going to change that.

While still young, she married her own brother, a man named Mausolus. Now that might seem very **weird**[3] to us today, but in those days, boys and girls were often raised separately, so it didn't seem odd to her.

In fact, she was madly in love with him, and he with her. They loved each other so much that people worried that if one of them died, the other would pine away, which means they would gradually die of sadness.

The truth would soon be known. Because Mausolus became sick and then he eventually did die.

✧✧✧

Artemisia was so crazy with grief that people far and wide commented on the strength of her love. Writers wrote about it in history books.

阿尔特米西娅（Artemisia）是一位公主。这是一个很酷的身份吗？可能不是。

在古代，公主一生中很少有自己选择的机会——她们甚至不能选择同谁结婚。爱情不是件值得认真考虑的事。

公主可以作为交易被皇室嫁给其他富有的家族，而浪漫与这桩交易无缘。

但卡里亚（位于现今的土耳其境内）的阿尔特米西娅二世却打算改变这一切。

她在很年轻的时候就嫁给了自己的哥哥摩索拉斯（Mausolus）。这种行为对于如今的我们来说是不可思议的，但在当时，男子和女子是分开抚养的，所以对于她来说这并不奇怪。

事实上，阿尔特米西娅疯狂地爱上了自己的哥哥，她的哥哥也是如此。他们互相深爱着，以至于人们担心如果其中一人去世，另一人会日益消瘦，最终也死于相思。

人们所担心的事还是发生了，摩索拉斯病倒了，最终不幸去世。

阿尔特米西娅悲伤得快要发疯了，人们到处谈论她这种深沉的爱情。作家把这件事写进了历史书中。

---

① **seal deal** 秘密交易、密封处理
② **turkey** [ˈtɜːkɪ] *n.* 土耳其
③ **weird** [wɪəd] *adj.* 怪异的、不可思议的、超自然的

She had her workers build a huge **monument**① for the body of Mausolus, and called it a **Mausoleum**②. His body was **cremated**③, and every day she put some of his ashes into a drink and drank it.

But Artemisia was now ruler of the land, and had some responsibilities. Her kingdom was at war with a neighboring place called Latmus. Her generals had fought hard with the soldiers of Latmus but had achieved nothing.

"Let me see what I can do," said Artemisia.

She announced that she and the royal ladies were going to organize the most **spectacular**④ meeting to **worship**⑤ the gods (everyone welcome!) at a particularly beautiful location in the countryside. There would be music and dancers and a **procession**⑥.

Large numbers of people came to join the spiritual gathering, including the men and women of Latmus. And as soon as they left their city gates, Artemisia's men quietly took over the place.

Many people said it was the sort of **trick**⑦ that would never have occurred to an army general, but was a smart move by a clever queen.

Artemisia was still sad, and each morning seemed to get weaker in spirit and body.

她让人们为摩索拉斯建造了一座巨大的纪念碑，将其命名为摩索拉斯陵墓。他的遗体被火化，阿尔特米西娅每天都要用他的骨灰泡水喝。

　　但是，阿尔特米西娅现在是这片领土的统治者，她有自己应尽的责任。她的王国和邻国拉特莫斯正在交战。她手下的将领们与敌国的士兵战斗得非常激烈，但还未收获辉煌的战果。

　　阿尔特米西娅说："让我看看我能做些什么。"

　　她对外宣告，她将和皇家贵妇们在美丽的郊外组织一场最华丽的盛典，以表达对上帝的崇拜之情。（欢迎任何人前来！）盛典上会有音乐、舞蹈和游行队伍。

　　许多人前来参加这次鼓舞人心的聚会，包括拉特莫斯国的男女。但他们一出自己的城门，阿尔特米西娅的将士们就占领了这座城池。

　　许多人都说，这真是个妙计！就连将领们都不可能想到的，这位聪明的女王却想到了。

　　阿尔特米西娅仍然很伤心，她的身心日复一日地虚弱。

① **monument**［'mɒnjʊm(ə)nt］*n.* 纪念碑、历史遗迹；*vt.* 为……树碑
② **mausoleum**［ˌmɔːsə'liəm］*n.* 陵墓、阴森森的大厦［mausoleums 或 mausolea］Mausoleum（摩索拉斯王陵）
③ **cremate**［krɪ'meɪt］*vt.* 火葬、烧成灰［cremated, cremated, cremating］
④ **spectacular**［spek'tækjʊlə］*adj.* 壮观的、惊人的，公开展示的［more spectacular, most spectacular］
⑤ **worship**［'wɜːʃɪp］*n.* 崇拜、礼拜、尊敬；*vt.* 崇拜、尊敬；*vi.* 拜神、做礼拜。［worshiped 或 -shipped，worshiped 或 -shipped，worshiping 或 -shipping］
⑥ **procession**［prə'seʃ(ə)n］*n.* 队伍、行列、一列、一排、列队行进；*vi.* 列队行进；*vt.* 沿着……行进
⑦ **trick**［trɪk］*n.* 诡计、恶作剧、花招、骗局；*vt.* 欺骗、哄骗；*vi.* 哄骗、戏弄

Her broken heart killed her in 350 BC, less than two years after the death of the man she loved. But even though she lived more than two **millennia**① ago, we still remember her as the princess who taught the world some important lessons about humanity.

Marriages are not just about linking families. She showed how powerful love can be, and she showed that what some people might call "female thinking" could achieve what "male thinking" might fail at.

And to this day, people around the world use her word, mausoleum, to talk about any building designed to enable people to remember a great and much-loved person who has died. Artemisia taught the world how to love.

公元前 350 年，在心爱的摩索拉斯去世后不到两年，她因伤心过度去世了。然而，即使 2000 多年过去了，我们仍然记得她，作为公主，她教会了全世界关于人性的重要道理。

结婚不只是两个家族的联姻。阿尔特米西娅证明了爱情的巨大力量，展示了被一些人称之为"女性思维"做到的事，这些事"男性思维"却做不到。

全世界的人们至今都在使用她的"摩索拉斯陵墓"一词，指代受人爱戴的伟人去世后、人们为了纪念他而设计的建筑。阿尔特米西娅教会了全世界所有人如何去爱。

---

① millennia [mɪˈleniə] n. 千年期、一千年、千年庆典、太平盛世

THE MOTHER WITH SIX BOYS AND SIX GIRLS

莉莉安·吉尔布雷斯
六个男孩和六个女孩的母亲

ERNESTINE AND FRANK WERE two English-speaking children who would come to the dinner table speaking French one day and German the next.

How come? That will be explained shortly.

Life was strange in their house. The pair would have a lot of people to practice their new languages with — because there were six boys and six girls in their family.

Yes! Twelve children in one family!

How did the parents manage? With difficulty, of course, since something as simple as a trip to a nearby playground would be extremely challenging to organize.

But the mum and dad of the Gilbreth family were amazing people. Mum (named Lillian) and Dad (named Frank) and their children lived in the USA and this true story took place about 100 years ago.

The amazing thing was that the Gilbreth parents were **specialists**[1] in engineering and science, but soon found a specialty to make their own: **efficiency**[2].

They became famous as efficiency experts, and many of today's ideas in **ergonomics**[3] (that's the science of achieving as much as possible with as little wasted effort as possible) came from their work. Lillian Gilbreth is now seen as the very first industrial psychologist.

Of course, people made a lot of jokes. It seemed as if the couple had had such a lot of children **deliberately**[4], to force themselves to be super-efficient every day of their lives!

欧内斯廷和弗兰克能够在第一天晚餐时说法语,第二天晚餐时说德语,然而他俩的母语是英语。

这是怎么做到的?解释起来很容易。

他们家的生活很特殊,家有六个男孩和六个女孩,所以欧内斯廷和弗兰克有机会和很多人一起练习新学到的语言。

是的!一个家庭中有 12 个孩子!

他们的父母如何管理这些孩子呢?当然困难重重,即使是组织一次去附近操场走走这样简单的活动,都非常具有挑战性。

这对父母——吉尔布雷斯夫妇——都是杰出的人物。母亲莉莉安·吉尔布雷斯(Lillian Gilbreth)、父亲弗兰克·吉尔布雷斯(Frank Gilbreth)和他们的孩子住在美国,这个真实的故事发生在大约 100 年前。

令人惊奇的是,吉尔布雷斯夫妇是工程和科学方面的专家,他们很快发现了自己的专长:高效率。

他们成了著名的效率专家,如今很多工效学(关于尽可能减少资源浪费,同时取得更好效果的科学)方面的观点均来源于他们的研究。如今莉莉安·吉尔布雷斯被认为历史上第一位工业心理学家。

当然,人们也开了很多玩笑:这对夫妇似乎是故意生下这么多孩子,以此来督促自己每天高效率地生活!

---

① **specialist** [ˈspeʃ(ə)lɪst] *n.* 专家
② **efficiency** [ɪˈfɪʃ(ə)nsɪ] *n.* 效率、效能、功效 [efficiencies]
③ **ergonomics** [ˌɜːɡəˈnɒmɪks] *n.* 工效学、人类工程学
④ **deliberately** [dɪˈlɪbərətlɪ] *adv.* 谨慎地、慎重地

Here are some examples. The mum, Lillian, worked out that people in kitchens moved in a **triangular**[①] shape, from the **sink**[②] to the cooker to the counter — and that information, when revealed in a book, became influential in kitchen design.

Another efficiency trick was to sometimes do two things at once. There would be language learning records playing in the bathroom while the children were using it — which explains why the youngsters would go to the bathroom to wash their hands, and then come to dinner speaking French and German.

When the family would go out, people would ask why they had so many children, and the Dad would joke: "It's cheaper by the dozen, you know." This was a standard line that sales people used in those days to encourage people to buy more items and get a discount.

When Ernestine and Frank, the two youngsters mentioned at the beginning of this report, grew up, they wrote a book about their hilarious family life. It was called "Cheaper by the Dozen".

The book has been made into a movie twice, the most recent one being a very funny film **starring**[③] Steve Martin — do take a look if you get the chance.

But don't forget: that oversized family really existed — and was responsible for some of the most important work in the science of efficiency.

这里有一些例子。母亲莉莉安计算得出：厨房里的人移动的位置形状是三角形，即从水槽到炊具再到料理台。当这一信息在一本书中披露出来后，对后来厨房的设计产生了很大的影响。

另一个关于效率的窍门是：同时做两件事。当孩子在盥洗室洗漱时，可以同时播放帮助孩子学习语言的磁带。这也解释了为什么年轻人先在盥洗室洗手，接着在晚餐时说法语和德语。

当全家出动外出游玩时，人们会问为什么他们家有这么多的孩子。这时父亲会开玩笑说："你懂的，一打更便宜。"一打也成为如今卖家鼓励人们买更多东西从而享受折扣的标准线。

当欧内斯廷和弗兰克，本故事开头提到的两个年轻人长大后，他们写了一本关于他们热闹的家庭生活的书。那本书叫作《儿女一箩筐》。

这本书被两次翻拍成电影，最近的一次是由著名喜剧明星史蒂夫·马丁（Steve Martin）出演的。如果有机会你可以去看看。

但请别忘记：这个超过一般规模的家庭确实存在过，并且对效率学的研究作出了重要的贡献。

---

① **triangular** [traɪˈæŋɡjʊlə] *adj.* 三角的、三角形的、三人间的
② **sink** [sɪŋk] *n.* 水槽、洗涤槽
③ **star** [stɑː] *vt.* 由……主演、由……担任主角；*vi.* 担任主角；[starred, starred, starring]

THE GIRL BORN IN THE SHADOW OF THE MOON GOD

恩西杜安娜
出生于月神之影中的女孩

ONCE UPON A TIME there was a beautiful princess who was the daughter of the **High Priestess**① of the Moon God and a great **warrior**② called King Sargon of Akkad.

That sounds like something out of a story book, right?

But in fact, that's a true story and exactly how history remembers a girl named Enheduanna (pronounced En-hed-u-ah-na).

She was born as the child of the High Priestess of the Moon God in a place which appears in history books as Mesopotamia.

Why? Because it may be one of the oldest female names in history. She was born in 2285 BC — more than four thousand years ago!

While there are lots of historical clues to what people were doing a long time ago, there are very few people whose names were written down, and the few who were, were nearly all men.

The name of her father, King Sargon, was written down, but **archeologists**③ are not sure about her mother's name. One explorer found a single piece of broken pot in the area with a name on it: Tashlultum. So that may have been the name of Enheduanna's mother. No one knows for sure.

Enheduanna was the name she took when she became a young adult and was **appointed**④ High Priestess of Innana, the goddess of love and war and wisdom and **lust**⑤ (what a combination!). Nobody knows what she was called when she was a small child.

从前有一位美丽的公主,是月神女祭司和古巴比伦阿卡德帝国的伟大战士萨贡王的女儿。

这听起来像是一本故事书中的情节,对不对?

但事实上,这是一个真实的故事,讲述历史如何铭记一个名叫恩西杜安娜(Enheduanna)的女孩。

作为月神女祭司的孩子,她出生在历史书中称为美索不达米亚的地方。

为什么这么说?因为恩西杜安娜可能是历史上最古老的女性名字了。她在公元前2285年出生——距今4000多年前!

尽管有大量的历史线索能够帮助我们了解古代人的日常生活,但很少有人的名字被记录下来,而为数不多的被记录下来的名字几乎都是男性。

她的父亲萨贡王的名字被记录了下来,但考古学家不能确定她母亲的名字。一位探险家在当地的一块破罐碎片上发现了一个名字:塔什纳特姆(Tashlultum),很可能就是恩西杜安娜母亲的名字。但没有人能确定。

恩西杜安娜是她在成年后被任命为昴宿星女祭司后取的名字,昴宿星是代表爱、战争、智慧和欲望的女神(多么奇妙的结合体啊!),没有人知道她小时候叫什么名字。

---

① **high priestess** 女祭司、女领袖
② **warrior** [ˈwɒrɪə] n. 战士、勇士
③ **archeologist** [ˌɑːkɪˈɒlədʒɪst] n. 考古学家
④ **appoint** [əˈpɔɪnt] vt. 任命、指定、约定;vi. 任命、委派
⑤ **lust** [lʌst] n. 强烈的欲望;vi. 贪求、渴望

But what she did that was important was to become a writer. She wrote poems and hymns and thoughtful essays about spiritual things. Her work survived and influenced many books through the ages. She may even be the earliest known author to have signed her books.

As a High Priestess, she had to help govern one of the regions of the country, which wasn't easy. At one time, she and her brother were **deposed**[①] and had to work hard to get back into power.

Enheduanna would have heard stories of a famous earlier ruler of the land, a man called Gilgamesh, who lived a couple of hundred years before her, and who was said to have had a friendship with a strange creature who was half-man, half-monster.

She may have started writing a book about him, or inspired other people to do so. Because one of the most famous books in the world has been traced back to about 2100 BC, which is not long after her death.

The stories of Gilgamesh were eventually compiled into humanity's earliest surviving work of literature, and may even be counted as the first novel ever.

If you like reading (or writing) stories, say thank you to one of humanity's first named authors, Enheduanna, daughter of the High Priestess of the Moon God.

她做的最重要的一件事是成了一名作家。她写诗、圣歌和关于心灵的思想性散文。她的作品流传下来,影响了一代又一代的书籍。她可能是已知最早的在书上署名的作家。

作为一名女祭司,她帮助管理一个地区,这并不容易。有一段时间,她和哥哥被免职,不得不努力工作才重新得到权势。

恩西杜安娜听说过这个国家早期的一位著名统治者吉尔伽美什(Gilgamesh)的故事,他生活在几百年前,据说和半人半怪的奇异生物交朋友。

她可能开始撰写一本关于吉尔伽美什的书,也可能是鼓励别人去写。因为世界上最著名的书籍之一可以追溯到公元前2100年左右,正是她去世后不久。

吉尔伽美什的故事最后汇编成了人类最早有记载的文学作品,后人甚至认为它是第一部小说。

如果你喜欢读(或写)故事,对月神女祭司的女儿恩西杜安娜说声谢谢吧,她是人类历史上第一位署名的作家。

---

① **depose** [dɪˈpəʊz] *vt.* 免职、废黜 [deposed, deposed, deposing]

THE EXPLORER GIRL WHO TRAVELLED FAR WITHOUT LEAVING HOME

爱丽丝·汉密尔顿
在家远行的探险女孩

A TEENAGE GIRL CALLED Alice sat on a chair, **gripped**[1] by a book.

It was called "The Merv Oasis", and it was the **thrilling**[2] true story of an explorer called Edmund O'Donovan who went to a land called Persia and met people of all sorts of cultures living dangerous lives on the edge of the desert.

It was a high-risk part of the world — shortly after writing the book, the author went on another **expedition**[3] and lost his life.

The girl **snapped**[4] the book shut and made up her mind.

She was going to be a medical **missionary**[5] and go to distant **exotic**[6] lands to help people in need.

Alice knew it would be difficult, since in those days, pretty much all doctors and explorers were men.

The first part of her plan went fine. Alice Hamilton, who had been born in 1869 in New York, successfully studied medicine and became a doctor. But where to go?

That's when she made a discovery.

There was no need to travel to exotic lands. There were plenty of people who needed her help in the poor areas of her own country.

In the early 1900s, factory workers, including children, were made to work on a range of items, including things made of lead and even radioactive materials!

一个名叫爱丽丝的年轻女孩端坐在椅子上,她被一本书吸引住了。

那本书的书名是《梅尔夫绿洲》,讲述的是一个名叫奥多诺万(Edmund O'Donovan)的冒险家惊心动魄的真实经历。他前往波斯,见识了各种文化背景的人在沙漠边缘的危险生活。

冒险的风险很大,那位作者在写完《梅尔夫绿洲》后不久就去了另一个地方探险,然而不幸丧命。

爱丽丝"啪"的一声合上书,作出了一个决定。

她决心成为一名医疗使者,去遥远的国度帮助有需要的人。

爱丽丝知道要当上医生很难,因为在那时,几乎所有的医生和探险家都是男性。

❧❧❧❧❧❧

她计划的第一步进行得很顺利。爱丽丝·汉密尔顿(Alice Hamilton)——1869年出生于纽约——如愿学习医学,成了一名医生。但她去哪里工作呢?

就在那时,她有了一个发现。

她发现没有必要去远方。在她自己的国家里,贫穷地区的很多人需要她的帮助。

在20世纪早期,工厂中的工人(包括童工)被迫接触以各种材料生产的产品,包括以铅甚至辐射性物品为原材料的产品!

① **grip** [ɡrɪp] vt. 紧握、夹紧;vi. 抓住
② **thrilling** ['θrɪlɪŋ] adj. 令人兴奋的、颤动的
③ **expedition** [ekspɪ'dɪʃ(ə)n] n. 远征、探险
④ **snap** [snæp] vt. 突然折断、拉断;vi. 咬、厉声说;n. 猛咬、噼啪声、突然折断[snapped, snapped, snapping]
⑤ **missionary** ['mɪʃ(ə)n(ə)rɪ] adj. 传教的、传教士的;n. 传教士。[missionaries]
⑥ **exotic** [ɪɡ'zɒtɪk; eɡ-] adj. 异国的、外来的,异国情调的

Alice Hamilton knew a lot about science and made a huge **fuss**[1].

Bosses were failing to keep their workers safe, she **thundered**[2].

Other people had been saying the same thing, but since Alice was a medical doctor, she could produce scientific proof that radiation killed people — so people started to listen.

※※※

Alice Hamilton became a world expert on **occupational health**[3], and her influence spread around the planet.

Once she ended up in a **courtroom**[4] trying to prove that something called "happy dust" that was being given to children was actually illegal **cocaine**[5]. So she dropped some into her eyes and showed the judges how it made the **pupils**[6] **dilate**[7], which means the black part at the center gets bigger.

※※※

Today, whether you work in a school or a factory or an office, there will be some sort of "health and safety **inspectors**[8]" who will make sure you won't be harmed by things around you.

Their existence was inspired by the work of Alice Hamilton and other occupational health experts. She changed the way society thinks about workers: it is now part of a boss's responsibility to make sure they are not putting their staff into **hazardous**[9] situations.

爱丽丝·汉密尔顿很懂科学,她掀起了一场轩然大波。

她指责工厂老板,说他们没有保障工人的安全。

其他人也说过同样的话,但因为爱丽丝是一位医生,她提供科学证据证明辐射会致人死亡,人们才开始对此有所反应。

爱丽丝·汉密尔顿成了职业健康方面的世界级专家,她的影响力遍及全球。

有一次,为了在法庭上证明孩子们收到的"幸福的灰尘"事实上是非法的可卡因,她洒了一些这种"灰尘"到自己的眼睛里,向法官证实它导致瞳孔扩张,眼睛中心的黑色部分变大了。

如今,无论你是在学校、工厂还是在办公室工作,那里都会有"健康安全督察员",确保你不被周遭的事物所伤害。

他们的存在源自爱丽丝·汉密尔顿和其他职业卫生健康专家的努力。爱丽丝改变了社会对于工人的认知:老板对工人的安全负有责任,必须确保工人不处于危险境地。

① **fuss** [fʌs] *vi.* 小题大做、无事自扰;*vt.* 使烦恼、使烦忧
② **thunder** ['θʌndə] *vi.* 打雷、怒喝;*vt.* 轰隆地发出、大声喊出
③ **occupational health** 职业健康,职业医疗保健
④ **courtroom** ['kɔːtruːm; -rʊm] *n.* 法庭、审判室
⑤ **cocaine** [kə(ʊ)'keɪn] *n.* 可卡因
⑥ **pupil** ['pjuːpɪl; -p(ə)l] *n.* 瞳孔
⑦ **dilate** [daɪ'leɪt; dɪ-] *vi.* 扩大、膨胀、详述;*vt.* 使扩大、使膨胀 [dilated, dilated, dilating]
⑧ **inspector** [ɪn'spektə] *n.* 检查员、巡视员
⑨ **hazardous** ['hæzədəs] *adj.* 有危险的、冒险的,碰运气的

She was the first woman to become a teacher at Harvard University, and in 1944, researchers decided to put her name on a famous list called "Men in Science"!

Even though she was a woman, she didn't mind. She knew that even though she had stayed in her own country, she had actually made a huge and important journey into an exotic place: she had entered a Man's World and she knew other women would follow.

For more on the same lines, check out other books in this series.

爱丽丝是哈佛大学第一位女教师。1944年，研究者决定将她的名字置于著名的"科学大师"名单上！

虽然是一名女性，但汉密尔顿并不介意自己的性别。她知道，尽管自己身处国内，但她已经到异域进行了一场伟大而重要的旅行：她进入了男性的世界，而其他女性必定会追随她的脚步。

如果想要知道更多这样的故事，您可以继续阅读本丛书的其他内容。

The Young Scientists Series:
Scientific Pioneers and The Science of Humanity

by

Nury Vittachi

English Copyright © 2017 by World Scientific Publishing Co. Pte. Ltd.

Bi-lingual (Simplified Chinese & English) Character Copyright © 2018 by Shanghai Scientific & Technological Education Publishing House

Shanghai Scientific & Technological Education Publishing House published bi-lingual edition by arranged with World Scientific Publishing Co. Pte. Ltd., Singapore

All rights reserved. This book, or parts thereof, may not be reproduced in any form or by any means, electronic or mechanical, including photocopying, recording or any information storage and retrieval system now known or to be invented, without written permission from the Publisher.

ALL RIGHTS RESERVED

上海科技教育出版社业经World Scientific Publishing Co. Pte. Ltd.同意取得本书中英文双语版版权

责任编辑　侯慧菊
封面设计　杨　静

"伟人的少年故事"丛书
科学的先驱——推动科学方法诞生的奇才
［斯里兰卡］努雷·维塔奇（Nury Vittachi）　著
斯泰帕·张（Step Cheung）　图
朱之翀　译
张　群　审校

出版发行	上海科技教育出版社有限公司
	（上海市柳州路218号　邮政编码200235）
网　　址	www.ewen.co　www.sste.com
经　　销	各地新华书店
印　　刷	上海昌鑫龙印务有限公司
开　　本	889×1194　1/32
印　　张	3
版　　次	2018年8月第1版
印　　次	2018年8月第1次印刷
书　　号	ISBN 978-7-5428-6713-1/G·3839
图　　字	09-2017-937号
定　　价	25.00元

扫描二维码
获取教师参考资料
及练习答案

扫描二维码
获取学生练习册